TRACE THE QURAN

A
CHILDREN'S BOOK

VOL.1

By Umm yahya

Dedicated to my daughter

Ayaam,

the brightest girl I know

Barakallahufeeha

Move your tongue. but not in haste

Though don't take long. this is a race

To see which ones are best in deeds

With pure intentions you will succeed

Learn The Quran. then go on and teach

There is no goal you cannot reach

For indeed Allah will raise your rank

For every breath you need to take

Know that every letter counts as ten

So while you listen. pick up your pen!

This book belongs to

____

بسم الله الرحمن الرحيم

Trace
me

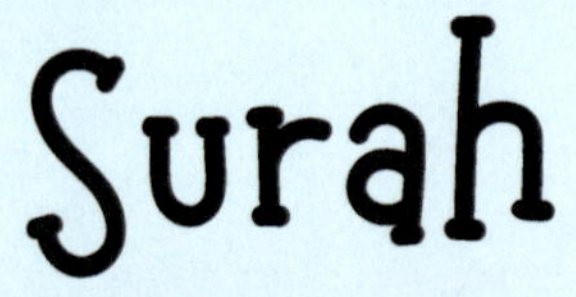

1. In the name of Allah, the Gracious, the Merciful. 2. Praise be to Allah, Lord of the Worlds. 3. The Most Gracious, the Most Merciful. 4. Master of the Day of Judgment. 5. It is You we worship, and upon You we call for help. 6. Guide us to the straight path. 7. The path of those You have blessed, not of those against whom there is anger, nor of those who are misguided.

بِسْمِ ٱللَّهِ ٱلرَّحْمَـٰنِ ٱلرَّحِيمِ ١ ٱلْحَمْدُ لِلَّهِ رَبِّ ٱلْعَـٰلَمِينَ ٢ ٱلرَّحْمَـٰنِ ٱلرَّحِيمِ ٣ مَـٰلِكِ يَوْمِ ٱلدِّينِ ٤ إِيَّاكَ نَعْبُدُ وَإِيَّاكَ نَسْتَعِينُ ٥ ٱهْدِنَا ٱلصِّرَٰطَ ٱلْمُسْتَقِيمَ ٦ صِرَٰطَ ٱلَّذِينَ أَنْعَمْتَ عَلَيْهِمْ غَيْرِ ٱلْمَغْضُوبِ عَلَيْهِمْ وَلَا ٱلضَّآلِّينَ ٧

SURAH AL FEEL

In the name of Allah, the Gracious, the Merciful
1. Have you not considered how your Lord dealt with the People of the Elephant? 2. Did He not make their plan go wrong? 3. He sent against them swarms of birds. 4. Throwing at them rocks of baked clay. 5. Leaving them like chewed-up leaves.

بِسْمِ اللَّهِ الرَّحْمَنِ الرَّحِيمِ

أَلَمْ تَرَ كَيْفَ فَعَلَ رَبُّكَ بِأَصْحَابِ الْفِيلِ ١ أَلَمْ يَجْعَلْ كَيْدَهُمْ فِي تَضْلِيلٍ ٢ وَأَرْسَلَ عَلَيْهِمْ طَيْرًا أَبَابِيلَ ٣ تَرْمِيهِم بِحِجَارَةٍ مِّن سِجِّيلٍ ٤ فَجَعَلَهُمْ كَعَصْفٍ مَّأْكُولٍ ٥

SURAH

AL QURAISH

In the name of Allah, the Gracious, the Merciful 1. For the security of Quraish. 2. Their security during winter and summer journeys. 3. Let them worship the Lord of this House. 4. Who has fed them against hunger, and has secured them against fear.

بِسْمِ اللَّهِ الرَّحْمَٰنِ الرَّحِيمِ

لِإِيلَٰفِ قُرَيْشٍ ١ إِۦلَٰفِهِمْ رِحْلَةَ الشِّتَآءِ

وَالصَّيْفِ ٢ فَلْيَعْبُدُوا رَبَّ هَٰذَا الْبَيْتِ

٣ الَّذِىٓ أَطْعَمَهُم مِّن جُوعٍ وَءَامَنَهُم

مِّنْ خَوْفٍۭ ٤

SURAH AL MA'UN

In the name of Allah, the Gracious, the Merciful 1. Have you considered him who denies the religion? 2. It is he who mistreats the orphan. 3. And does not encourage the feeding of the poor. 4. So woe to those who pray. 5. Those who are heedless of their prayers. 6. Those who put on the appearance. 7. And withhold the assistance.

بِسْمِ ٱللَّهِ ٱلرَّحْمَٰنِ ٱلرَّحِيمِ

أَرَءَيْتَ ٱلَّذِى يُكَذِّبُ بِٱلدِّينِ ١ فَذَٰلِكَ ٱلَّذِى يَدُعُّ ٱلْيَتِيمَ ٢ وَلَا يَحُضُّ عَلَىٰ طَعَامِ ٱلْمِسْكِينِ ٣ فَوَيْلٌ لِّلْمُصَلِّينَ ٤ ٱلَّذِينَ هُمْ عَن صَلَاتِهِمْ سَاهُونَ ٥ ٱلَّذِينَ هُمْ يُرَآءُونَ ٦ وَيَمْنَعُونَ ٱلْمَاعُونَ ٧

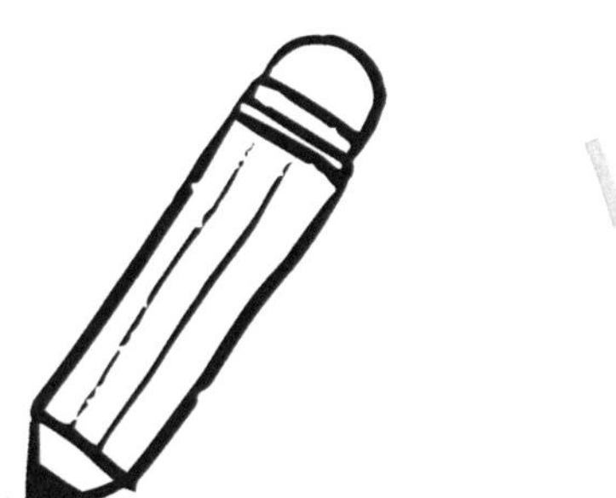

Surah Al-Kawthar

In the name of Allah, the Gracious, the Merciful
1. We have given you plenty.
2. So pray to your Lord and sacrifice. 3. He who hates you is the loser

بِسْمِ اللَّهِ الرَّحْمَٰنِ الرَّحِيمِ

إِنَّا أَعْطَيْنَٰكَ ٱلْكَوْثَرَ ١ فَصَلِّ لِرَبِّكَ وَٱنْحَرْ ٢ إِنَّ شَانِئَكَ هُوَ ٱلْأَبْتَرُ ٣

SURAH AL KAAFIROON

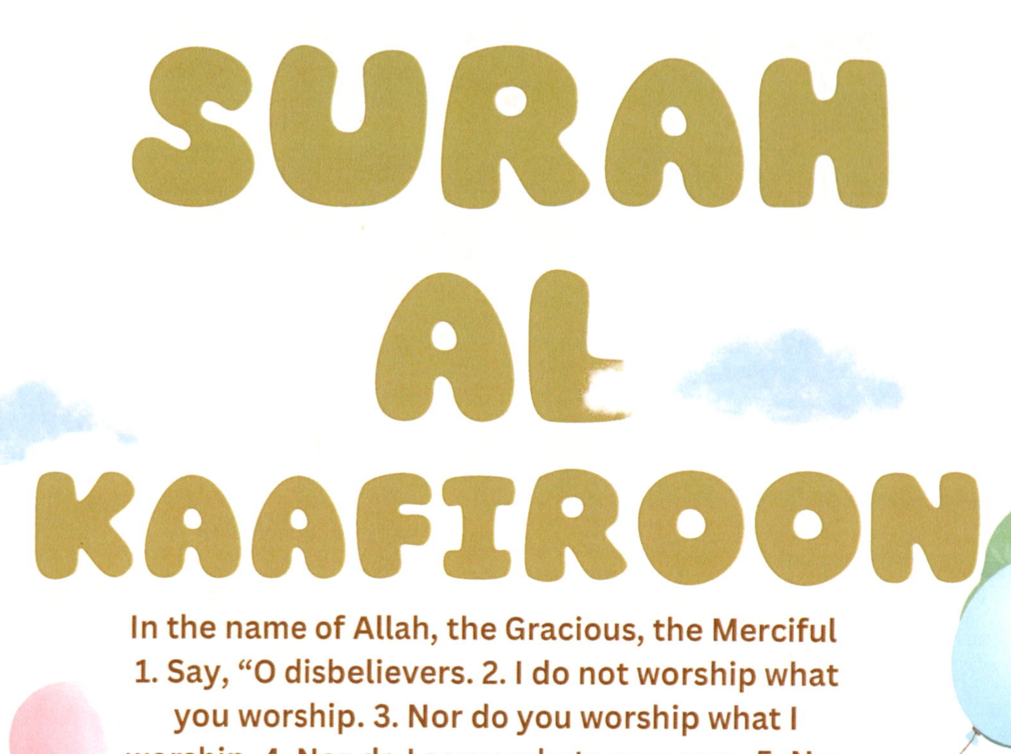

In the name of Allah, the Gracious, the Merciful
1. Say, "O disbelievers. 2. I do not worship what you worship. 3. Nor do you worship what I worship. 4. Nor do I serve what you serve. 5. Nor do you serve what I serve. 6. You have your way, and I have my way."

بِسْمِ اللهِ الرَّحْمٰنِ الرَّحِيمِ

قُلْ يَـٰٓأَيُّهَا ٱلْكَـٰفِرُونَ ١ لَآ أَعْبُدُ مَا تَعْبُدُونَ ٢ وَلَآ أَنتُمْ عَـٰبِدُونَ مَآ أَعْبُدُ ٣ وَلَآ أَنَا۠ عَابِدٌ مَّا عَبَدتُّمْ ٤ وَلَآ أَنتُمْ عَـٰبِدُونَ مَآ أَعْبُدُ ٥ لَكُمْ دِينُكُمْ وَلِىَ دِينِ ٦

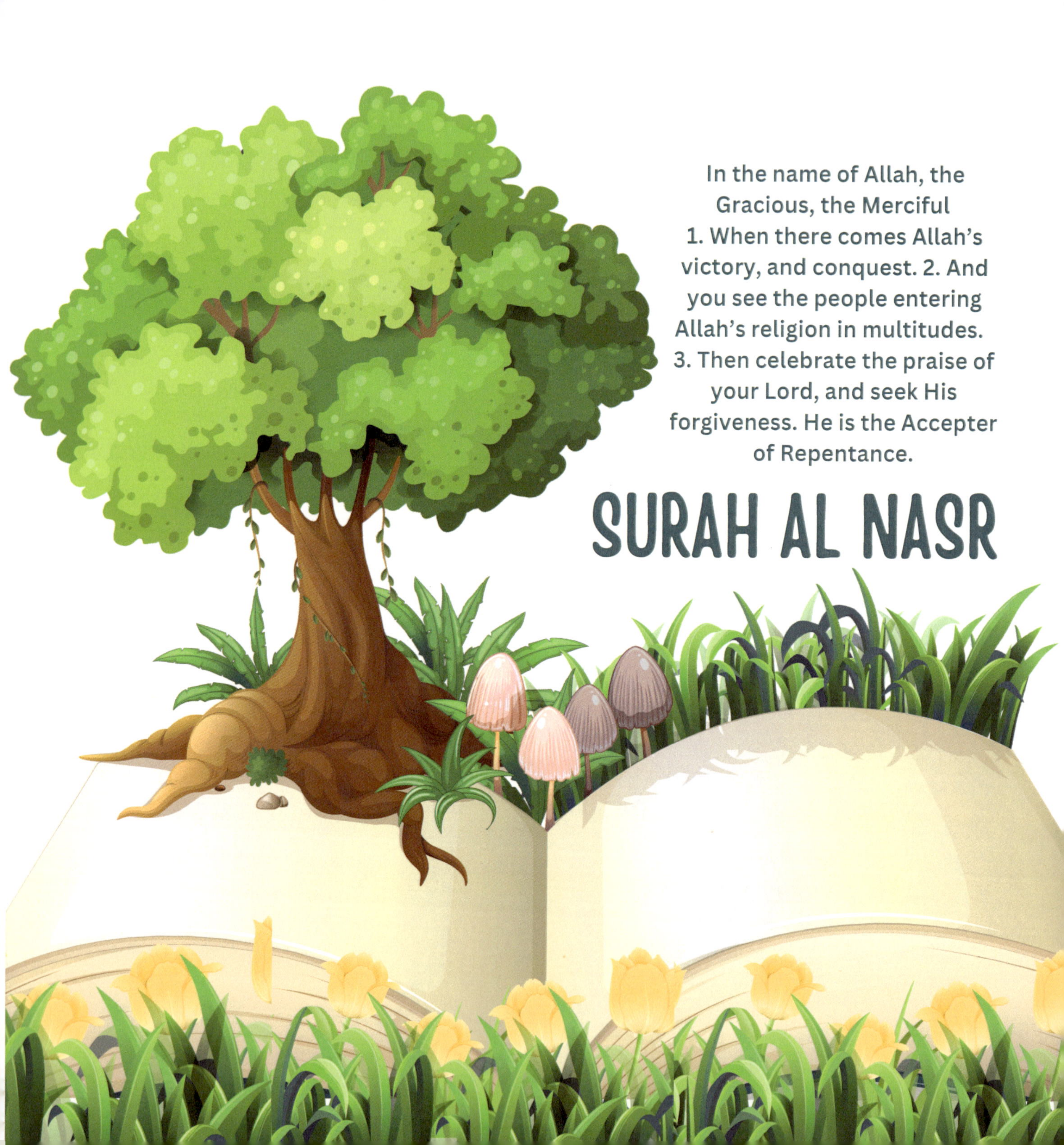

In the name of Allah, the Gracious, the Merciful
1. When there comes Allah's victory, and conquest. 2. And you see the people entering Allah's religion in multitudes. 3. Then celebrate the praise of your Lord, and seek His forgiveness. He is the Accepter of Repentance.
SURAH AL NASR

بِسْمِ اللَّهِ الرَّحْمَٰنِ الرَّحِيمِ

إِذَا جَآءَ نَصْرُ اللَّهِ وَالْفَتْحُ ١ وَرَأَيْتَ النَّاسَ يَدْخُلُونَ فِى دِينِ اللَّهِ أَفْوَاجًا ٢ فَسَبِّحْ بِحَمْدِ رَبِّكَ وَاسْتَغْفِرْهُ إِنَّهُ كَانَ تَوَّابًا ٣

SURAH AL MASAD

In the name of Allah, the Gracious, the Merciful 1. Condemned are the hands of Abee Lahab, and he is condemned. 2. His wealth did not avail him, nor did what he acquired. 3. He will burn in a Flaming Fire. 4. And his wife—the firewood carrier. 5. Around her neck is a rope of thorns.

بِسْمِ اللَّهِ الرَّحْمَٰنِ الرَّحِيمِ

تَبَّتْ يَدَآ أَبِى لَهَبٍ وَتَبَّ ١ مَآ أَغْنَىٰ عَنْهُ مَالُهُۥ وَمَا كَسَبَ ٢ سَيَصْلَىٰ نَارًا ذَاتَ لَهَبٍ ٣ وَٱمْرَأَتُهُۥ حَمَّالَةَ ٱلْحَطَبِ ٤ فِى جِيدِهَا حَبْلٌ مِّن مَّسَدٍ ٥

SURAH AL IKHLAS

In the name of Allah, the Gracious, the Merciful
1. Say, "He is Allah, the One. 2. Allah, the Absolute.
3. He begets not, nor was He begotten 4. And
there is nothing comparable to Him."

بِسْمِ اللَّهِ الرَّحْمَٰنِ الرَّحِيمِ

قُلْ هُوَ اللَّهُ أَحَدٌ ١ اللَّهُ الصَّمَدُ ٢

لَمْ يَلِدْ وَلَمْ يُولَدْ ٣ وَلَمْ يَكُن لَّهُ

كُفُوًا أَحَدٌ ٤

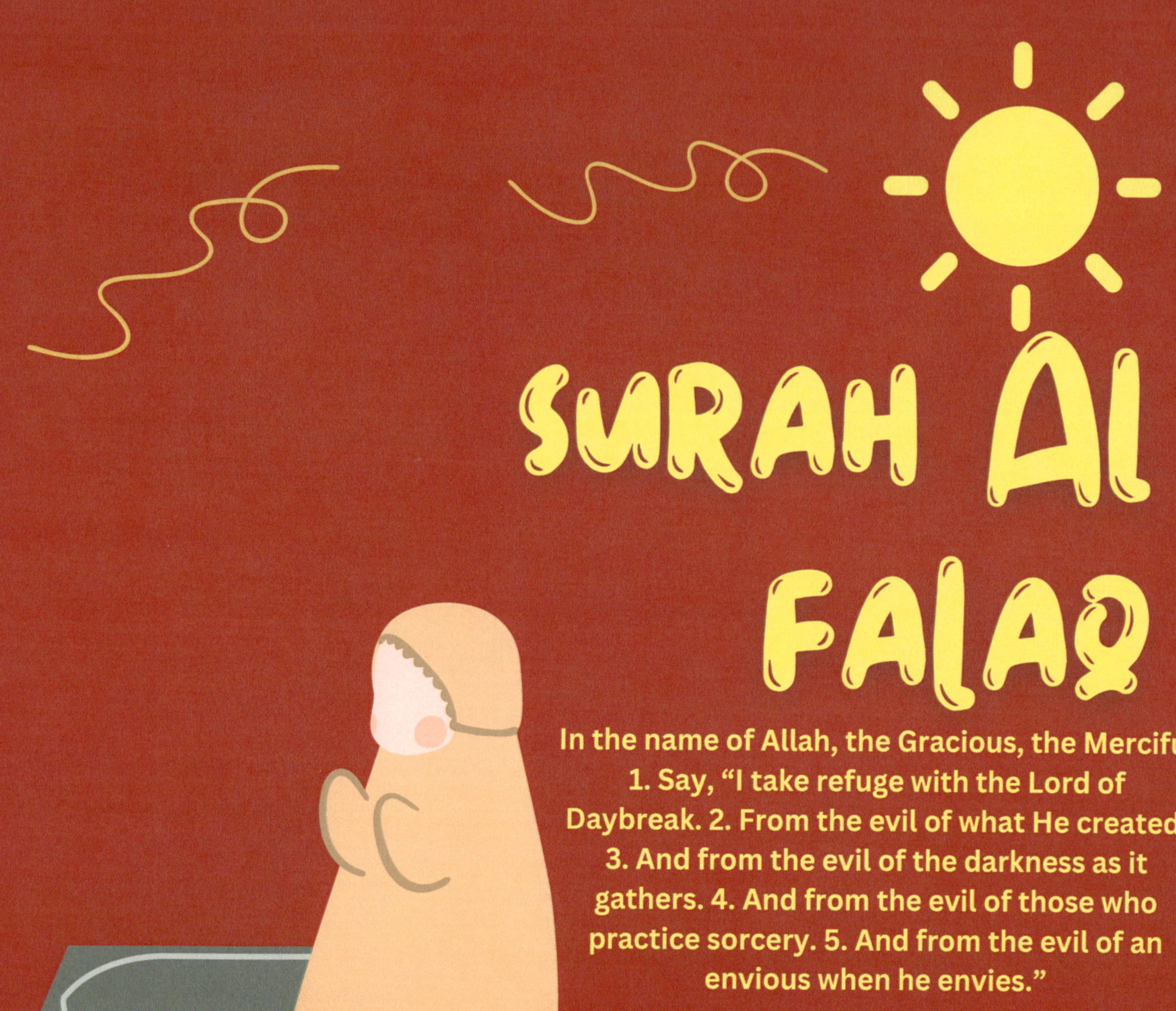

SURAH AL FALAQ

In the name of Allah, the Gracious, the Merciful 1. Say, "I take refuge with the Lord of Daybreak. 2. From the evil of what He created. 3. And from the evil of the darkness as it gathers. 4. And from the evil of those who practice sorcery. 5. And from the evil of an envious when he envies."

بِسْمِ اللَّهِ الرَّحْمَٰنِ الرَّحِيمِ

قُلْ أَعُوذُ بِرَبِّ الْفَلَقِ ١ مِن شَرِّ مَا خَلَقَ ٢ وَمِن شَرِّ غَاسِقٍ إِذَا وَقَبَ ٣ وَمِن شَرِّ النَّفَّاثَاتِ فِي الْعُقَدِ ٤ وَمِن شَرِّ حَاسِدٍ إِذَا حَسَدَ ٥

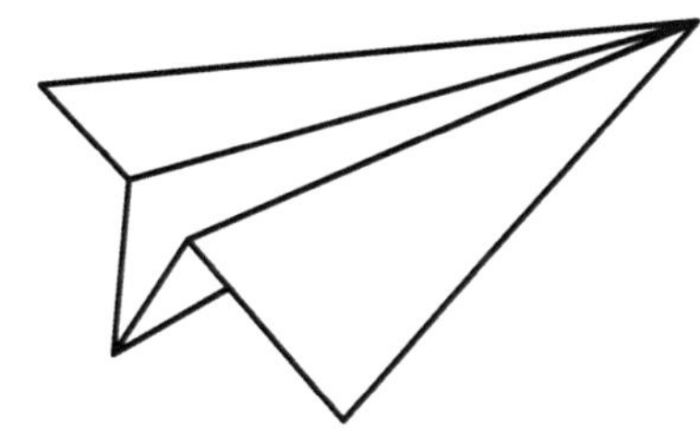

SURAH AL NAAS

In the name of Allah, the Gracious, the Merciful 1. Say, "I seek refuge in the Lord of mankind. 2. The King of mankind. 3. The God of mankind. 4. From the evil of the sneaky whisperer. 5. Who whispers into the hearts of people. 6. From among jinn and among people."

بِسْمِ اللهِ الرَّحْمَنِ الرَّحِيمِ

قُلْ أَعُوذُ بِرَبِّ ٱلنَّاسِ ١ مَلِكِ ٱلنَّاسِ ٢ إِلَٰهِ ٱلنَّاسِ ٣ مِنْ شَرِّ ٱلْوَسْوَاسِ ٱلْخَنَّاسِ ٤ ٱلَّذِى يُوَسْوِسُ فِى صُدُورِ ٱلنَّاسِ ٥ مِنَ ٱلْجِنَّةِ وَٱلنَّاسِ ٦

Dua For Knowledge

Exalted is Allah, the True King. Do not be hasty with the Quran before its inspiration to you is concluded, and say,

MY LORD! INCREASE ME IN KNOWLEDGE.

Ta'Ha: 114

Ameen